YOUR KNOWLEDGE HAS VALUE

- We will publish your bachelor's and
  master's thesis, essays and papers

- Your own eBook and book -
  sold worldwide in all relevant shops

- Earn money with each sale

Upload your text at www.GRIN.com
and publish for free

Sukayna El-Zayat

Bloody Diversity - State formation and Nation building in England

GRIN Verlag

Bibliografische Information der Deutschen Nationalbibliothek:

Die Deutsche Bibliothek verzeichnet diese Publikation in der Deutschen National-
bibliografie; detaillierte bibliografische Daten sind im Internet über http://dnb.d-
nb.de/ abrufbar.

Dieses Werk sowie alle darin enthaltenen einzelnen Beiträge und Abbildungen
sind urheberrechtlich geschützt. Jede Verwertung, die nicht ausdrücklich vom
Urheberrechtsschutz zugelassen ist, bedarf der vorherigen Zustimmung des Verla-
ges. Das gilt insbesondere für Vervielfältigungen, Bearbeitungen, Übersetzungen,
Mikroverfilmungen, Auswertungen durch Datenbanken und für die Einspeicherung
und Verarbeitung in elektronische Systeme. Alle Rechte, auch die des auszugsweisen
Nachdrucks, der fotomechanischen Wiedergabe (einschließlich Mikrokopie) sowie
der Auswertung durch Datenbanken oder ähnliche Einrichtungen, vorbehalten.

Imprint:

Copyright © 2012 GRIN Verlag GmbH
Druck und Bindung: Books on Demand GmbH, Norderstedt Germany
ISBN: 978-3-656-35288-4

This book at GRIN:

http://www.grin.com/en/e-book/206629/bloody-diversity-state-formation-and-
nation-building-in-england

GRIN - Your knowledge has value

Der GRIN Verlag publiziert seit 1998 wissenschaftliche Arbeiten von Studenten, Hochschullehrern und anderen Akademikern als eBook und gedrucktes Buch. Die Verlagswebsite www.grin.com ist die ideale Plattform zur Veröffentlichung von Hausarbeiten, Abschlussarbeiten, wissenschaftlichen Aufsätzen, Dissertationen und Fachbüchern.

Visit us on the internet:

http://www.grin.com/

http://www.facebook.com/grincom

http://www.twitter.com/grin_com

-Bloody Diversity -

State formation and Nation building in England

Sukayna El-Zayat
Date: 12.12.2012
Bloody Diversity
Final Version

Table of Contents

Introduction

Today, England is well integrated in Europe, being an active member of the European Union – nevertheless, keeping their distance to the continent, by e.g. insisting on their own currency and units. The English themselves state that the English people existed from the 'beginning of time' (Duffy, 2001) and indeed the population of the British Isles has roots back to the Roman Era. However, whether the idea of England is as old as that remains questionable. It most certainly was neither a state nor a nation at that time.

This paper deals with the process of state formation and nation building in England from the high Middle Ages until the end of the nineteenth century. Furthermore, it discusses whether England had been first a state or a nation or if this process occurred concurrently. It aims to determine when, how and why these developments proceeded in England the way they did, and if England's changes differed from the rest of Europe. This paper claims that in the case of England, state and nation building went hand in hand resulting in an early English nation-state. The rise of a national consciousness as well as the establishment of a sovereign state protecting individual rights would not have been possible without the early formation of parliament. Therefore, this paper argues that the evolvement of Parliament was essential and played a crucial role in shaping England into a nation state.

The notions of State, Nation and Nation States are historically and socially constructed, rather than being naturally developed phenomenons. (Palmer,1995).Furthermore, there exists a vast array of diverse definitions of those notions. Each definition seems to have certain shortcoming and this entails the necessity to connect different elements of those definitions in order to create a common ground for analysis. In the first section, this paper demonstrates the period of feudal England, describing what feudalism was and analyzing how it looked like in England. Next, after discussing different definitions of the state, the development of parliament in regard to the concept of sovereignty will be examined as well as nuances of absolutism in England. Afterwards, this paper focuses on nation building and takes position in the Warwick debate. Lastly, it refers to the idea of a nation state and gives a brief outline of the following developments of England as it completed its transformation into a modern nation state.

Feudal England

When William the Duke of Normandy seized power and crowned himself king, after defeating the Anglo-Saxon ruler in the battle of Hastings in 1066, he brought feudalism to England. The feudal system on the continent was originally an attempt by Charlemagne to recreate the Roman Empire or at least a comparable power.

Opello (1999), explains the concept of feudalism as followed. Feudalism is a distribution of power – the lord, in this case the king, chooses nobles who were loyal to him and made them his vassals. This meant that he gave them the right over certain amounts of land and everything that was on this land, including peasants. Moreover, the vassal was given judicial control over his territory; therefore, he collected the taxes from his subjects. In return, the lord could depend on three forms of support; firstly the vassal was obligated to provide military forces when the lord asked for them. Secondly, all vassals were committed to pay taxes to the lord; financial support. Lastly, the vassals formed a council in order to help their lord decide in political matters; for example whether to start a war or not. These reciprocate duties were guaranteed through a bound contract by life between lord and vassal. Since the vassals were in charge of all matters concerning their territory, they became very powerful and ruled directly over 'their' people. Consequently, the lord's influence on people was in reality next to nothing. Therefore, his vassals could become more powerful than the king.

The feudal system relied solely on personal ties between the lord and his vassals. Although officially a king reigned over a certain territory, there was actually no English state (the characteristics of a sovereign state are explained in the next section) – when the vassals swore allegiance to the king, they did it to him as an individual not to some abstract idea of a state. In fact, on the first look, the feudal system itself was not a step towards state building, but an attempt to restore an Empire. The king was not able to act as a central authority. Instead the medieval plurality of power led to an increased decentralization of power. (Opello, 1999, pp. 78)

Concept of Sovereignty

The most common and generally applicable definition of the state is provided by Simon Roberts, who defines the sovereign state as consisting of four elements, namely "a presence of a **supreme authority (1.),** ruling over a **defined territory (2.),** who is **recognized (3.)** as having power to make decisions in matters of government and **is able to enforce (4.)** such decisions and generally maintain order within the state" (Hall,1984, p.1).

These characteristics were not yet fulfilled by the feudal state as it lacked a central authority, an army belonging to the state and since each vassal ruled over his own relatively little piece of land - there was no defined territory either.

Precondition of a sovereign state had to be some kind of administrative centralization. In the process of depersonalizing governing, two separate systems were established. Financial institutions emerged, accountants were educated and a direct system of revenue collection through the sheriffs was set up. Moreover, a legal system emerged; professions as lawyers and judges materialized and courts were established. On the continent, pre-state entities tried to reinstate Roman Law as monarchs created legal codes as a set of rules. In England however, the legal system relied on common law. This meant that judges decided case by case and slowly precedent cases developed. From these a coherent legal set of rules could evolve. (Opello, 1999, pp.54).

In regard to the shift from the medieval state structure towards establishing sovereignty, two more aspects were significant; on the one hand the military development and on the other hand the English Protestant Reformation and its implications.

In most countries on the continent the military revolution played a major key role towards the transition into a modern, sovereign state (Palmer, 1995) Although the military revolution was not that present in England there were some basic approaches especially after the English Civil War. The wave of new military inventions did not skip England, and up to 1642 the British navy became an established power which made the Civil War possible in the first place. (Braddick, 1993, p. 965). Until that point of time, English military manpower had been more than doubled compared to the late sixteenth century. (Parker, 1976).

Apart from the military development, the transformation of the medieval state of the estates was pushed by the countless religious wars and conflicts which fragmented all of Europe and were mostly provoked by the Reformation. In England, religious reformation manifested itself mainly through the separation of the Anglican Church. King Henry VIII declared himself and all of his successors Head of the Church of England through the Act of Supremacy in 1534. The main reason for Henry to reject Rome was his wish to annul his marriage to Catherine of Argon as she was not able to give him a male heir. The pope, as head of the Catholic Church, did not support this request and therefore refused to execute the annulment. Although Queen Mary invalidated the Act after her fathers death as she was catholic, Queen Elizabeth 1, her half-sister reinstated herself as Supreme Governor and lead the English church. Smith however argues that Henry VIII breach with the papacy was not the beginning of English Protestantism, but that the movement had started before and that Luther did influence many English humanists. An example would be the early translation of the New Testament by William Tyndale (Smith, 1984, p. 15).

In a sovereign state, the concept of governing shifted from the system of a lord 'owning' his vassals towards the so-called raison d'état; meaning that the state consists of not only the crown but additionally the people and the land. It has its own specific interests and the 'art of government […] [lies] in recognizing those interests and necessities and acting in accordance with them…' (Craig, 1990, p.5). In consequence, the head of state must not primarily be seen as a person but as an authority representing the unity of the state. The Head of State had therefore almost an institutional character, which should consequently not be attached to a mortal and evanescent human body. During the reign of Elizabeth I this inner conflict of the monarch has been described as the dual nature of the king's body; '…For the king has in him two bodies, a Body natural and a Body politic'. (Kantorowicz, 1957). The Body natural refers simply to the actual, physical body of the king, being mortal and influenced by external powers. The Body politic however had to be separated from that. As Opello points out, it symbolized the bridge between the state's people and God, pillared by the monarch. (Opello, 1999, p.55).

The first time in Europe that the principle of state sovereignty was acknowledged and a Balance of Power between the different states emerged was during the peace of Westphalia. Originally it was established after the 30-years-war to avoid future wars. Although England did not take part in that war, the treaty was important considering the case of England as the sovereignty of each state, including Britain, was mutually recognized within the treaties of Westphalia.

Struggle between kingdom and baronage

When the vassal's power grew stronger, that was the beginning of a struggle of power between the crown and the nobility, the second of the three estates of the feudal society (clergy and bourgeoisie [mainly merchants] being the other two). In 1100, under the reign of Henry I , the king established an efficient financial system and developed a central administration. He still recognized the nobility and their rights, but he employed sheriffs who collected the taxes from the vassal more effectively (Opello, 1999, p.78). When he died in 1135, leaving no male heir, a dynastic war about the line of succession broke out. Without an active crown, the baronage grew stronger. Territorial conflicts and disputes between the nobles lead to a fragmented kingdom. In 1199, King John, who had to fight high inflation, increased taxes and demanded extremely high payments from the landlords. The following baronial revolt caused the creation of the Magna Charta (1215). This treaty was an enormous advantage for the baronage, since it granted them the right to assemble, an expansion of the counsel function and obliged the king not to collect taxes without the consent of the barons.

After this victory, barons forbade the king's sheriffs to enter their premises. John's successor, Henry III reorganized the council of barons and introduced a 'Model Parliament' (Opello, 1999, p.79). Apart from the baronage, members of the clergy, two knights for each region as well as two leading citizens were divided in the House of Lords and the House of Commons. In the following years, the parliament met regularly and acquired control over the royal ministers, finances (parliament evolved to a steady revenue for the crown) and even the military forces, because soldiers were still provided by the barons, so that the king was not able to build up a strong standing army.

Different shades of Absolutism

Coming back to the concept of Sovereignty is usually linked to the notion of absolutism. Whether England can be considered as an absolutist state depends on the applied definition of absolutism. Merriman defines certain characteristics of absolutist states; monarchial authority, centralized bureaucracy (revenue) and a large standing army (Merriman, 1996). Those characteristics are quite similar to the ones given by Roberts concerning sovereignty. Merriman argues furthermore that absolutism was in general the answer to a by war fragmented state. According to him, England was not an absolute state. Although one can consequently safely state that England was at least the state in Europe with the weakest manifestation of absolutism, it was home to Thomas Hobbes, a strong supporter of the absolutistic system. In his Leviathan (1651), Hobbes argues that absolutism is the only governmental system which is able to protect the human from its state of nature. According to him, in this state of nature, man fights against man and anarchy and chaos reign over the people. Hobbes therefore discusses the need for a social contract in which the subjects give up their rights in exchange for protection.

Opello argues that England in fact was influenced by the concept of absolutism as he presents England as a parliamentary absolutist state, referring to the institution of parliament as the absolutist power.(p.88). This approach is supported by the events of the Glorious Revolution, starting with the Civil War.

The English Civil War, which occurred from 1642 until 1648, established the parliament as an independent sovereign institution. Charles I needed money to calm rebellions in Scotland and Ireland; since the parliament did not agree to that, he imposed heavy taxes without their consent and tried to dissolve the parliament. The following Civil War against the crown resulted in Charles I being executed and the foundation of an English republic.   However, since the new republic was not able to stabilize its government, in 1660 English monarchy was restored. James II (ruled from 1685 onwards) planned to bring England back to Catholicism; he built up a standing army relying mostly on privateers – therefore strengthening the merchants and the gentry. This might seem as a setback for parliament, but in fact, through empowering the bourgeoisie and aiming to bypass the parliament, in the long-term he actually strengthened the nobility. The growing political importance of the bourgeoisie led than to an even more powerful parliament. Provoked by James II absolutist ambitions, parliament asked William of Orange to intervene. James II was banned into exile, and William III became king of England. In the Act of Settlement he accepted the crown under the conditions provided by parliament. Though still officially a monarchy, during this 'Glorious Revolution', parliament showcased their absolute power – being the sovereign of the emerging modern English state.

Nation building and nationalism

Anthony Smith defines the nation as such: "A named human population sharing an historic territory, common myths and memories, a mass-public-culture, a single economy and common rights and duties for all members". (Smith, 1996, pp..358). Hence, Smith uses an ethno-symbolic approach as he emphasizes the importance of values and memories in defining a nation. Furthermore, Smith proclaims that nationalism is characterized as an ideological, active movement and not merely a development. He states that it is essential for maintaining the autonomy and unity as well as identity of a state's population. Additionally, Smith derives certain 'symbolic goals' which often come hand in hand with the concept of nationalism. The first one is language education, as nationalists usually attempt to manifest one single language for one nation. Another one is the preservation of ancient sites together with tradition building in general. In order to create or maintain a national consciousness, a nation must be able to refer to a common myth or tradition. Therefore, many nationalistic historians tend to portrait specific historical events in a certain point of view which implies that this nation's characteristics are deeply rooted in 'their' history. By including this aspect, Smith indicates the subsequentness of nationalism, stating that "everything is caused by something ". (Smith,1996, p.364). He therefore incorporates early ethnical origins and roots of a nation in his approach.

However, scholars are not in agreement in regard to the definitions and some even contradict each other. As a result, one is faced just like it is the case for the state, with a diversity of definitions for nation and nationalism. The vivid debate surrounding this variety of definitions is known as the Warwick debate. The most important protagonists of this debate are on the one hand Anthony Smith and as his counterpart, on the other hand, Ernest Gellner.

Gellner states that "nationalism engendered the nation and not the other way round" (Gellner, 1994, p.56). Disagreeing with Smith, he indicates that nationalism is merely a result of specific modern changes. (Zimmer, 2003, p.5) He defines nationalism as "...the consequence of a new form of social organization, based on deeply internalized, education-dependent high cultures, each protected by its own state."(Gellner, 1983, p.63). He highlights the necessity of specific materialistic conditions such as industrialization, literacy in one common language and an educational system without which nationalism and therefore a nation would not emerge. He argues that nationalism is a product of cultural, economic and scientific changes only from the seventeenth century onwards and therefore matches the modern era. Gellner follows a more general, modernist approach. He denies the subsequentness defined by Smith as he states that the "knowledge of the past is too doubtful to trace back origins" (Smith, 1996, p.362) and consequently a theory on the emergence of nations and nationalism can only be generated at a very general level.

In order to understand those partly contradicting opinions one could consider Ernest Renan's definition which is in accordance with Gellner's position but still explains Smith' opinion. He formulates a definition as such: "A Nation presumes a past, but this past is summed up in (...) the agreement and the desire to continue a life in common" (Renan, 1996, p.52).

As Smith does not deny that the nation is more an artificial construct than a natural development, but rather expands Gellner's view and includes early roots before the seventeenth century, I find his approach more convincing. He criticizes the focus on modernity of Gellner, as it lacks to take pre-modern ethnic ties and memories into account. Furthermore, Gellner's theory could be denunciated for being too general, as it is too abstract to be applied on specific cases. Moreover, the modernists approach ties nationalism to industrial and economic conditions, which leaves out differently developed areas such as poorer countries and is for that reason misleading. As Smith claims; nationalism can emerge in all kinds of socio-economic milieus.

Schulze supports Smith but nonetheless managed to find a relatively accurate compromise within his definition: "Nations come to know themselves through their common history, their common reputation and the sacrifices they have made in common. It ought to be added, that their common history as a rule has no more than limited reality, it is more the product of dreams and visions than the product of facts" (Schulze, 1996, p.98). He refers to the nationalistic tradition of seeking historical evidence for certain aspects which are the assumed or wished for characteristics of that particular nation.

Concerning the case of England, one can find basic, nationalistic roots already in the fourteenth century which intensified later in the seventeenth century, especially under Tudor reign. Consequently, a mixture of Gellner and Smith fits the nation formation of England most appropriately.

An English national consciousness emerged in the middle of the fourteenth century for the first time. English as the common language of the people, unifying linguistic ties, manifested itself when in 1362 the English parliament began to hold its public meetings in English. (Kohn, 1940, pp.71) This development had been delayed through the influence of the French language, imported during the Norman conquest. And French still remained the lingua franca in Literature and Philosophies. England's self-awareness as a nation was pushed by the retreat from the continent after its defeat at the end of the Hundred-years-war. (Kohn, 1940, p.78). So the country's political loss was actually a step forward considering the formation of an English nation for instance as the English people now concentrated on their peculiarity caused by the insular situation. Additionally, Kohn (1940) explains that, at the time, several internal conflicts within the baronage, summarized as the War of the Roses, took place (p.83). In combination with the rise of the former third estate, this led to a heightened unification of the English people and therefore a national self-recognition. The decisive steps towards a unified English nation were taken under Tudor reign, beginning with Henry VIII. Through the installment of the Model Parliament, public opinion gained more importance in regard to political decision processes. A feeling of self-confidence and self-reliance arose and led to the materialization of a national homogeneity. When Henry VIII separated the English Protestant Church from the Roman Catholic Church this had naturally considerable consequences on the national consciousness. This action intensified the feeling of belongingness as well as the sentiment that the common English people were 'something special'. This understanding was strengthened as Queen Elizabeth seized power and England developed into the English Empire.

That was the time when the phenomenon of patriotism emerged. The national pride is mirrored for instance culturally as more and more writers produced the nation praising books such as Britannia by William Camden. (Kohn, 1940, p.72). John Lyly even compares England to "…a new Israel…" (Lyly, 1902, p.205), a promised land. This ambiance fell together with an economic and political growth, based on the strong navy and commerce, as the ground was set for England's transformation towards the great British Empire 'where the sun never sets'. Concurring mainly with Spain and Portugal, England acquired sea domination and conquered colonies overseas. At the Empires peak of power English territories covered about one-fifth of the world's population (Maddison, 2001,p.98). Those successes engendered a new consciousness. The common English people identified itself as bearers of history and at the same time builders of their own destiny (Kohn, 1940, p.74). Furthermore, this was the time where national constructivism is clearly apparent. The English added meaning and the notion of heritage to historical concepts; such as the English common law which supposedly led to the tradition of liberty.

The idea of a Nation-state

If the state can be defined as a political entity and the nation as a cultural and ethnic entity, then the nation-state describes the combination of those two concepts. If they overlap within a defined territory, than this area can be defined as a nation-state. Kumar describes it, as the "commitment to the state shared by rulers and ruled alike" (Kumar, 2003). Max Weber puts it similarly: "the nation-state is the nation's secular organization of power" (Zimmer, 2003).

Meineke subdivides the idea into two opposing concepts: the cultural nation on the one hand and the political nation on the other hand. The cultural nation, 'Kulturnation', is based on the community as a whole which is more important and superior to the individual. The people are connected through a common language, cultural tradition and historical heritage. This implies that one could only be a valid member of the community if one was born into it. Within this concept, there is the possibility that a nation could exist without a state. A historical example for this kind was Germany for instance. The notion of superiority and the idea of "Du bist nichts, dein Volk ist alles" (You are nothing, your community is everything) are characteristic and demonstrate the unimportance of the individual and its will. The political nation however can be applied to the case of England. According to this approach, the nation equals the state. Individual rights and freedoms act as the most important force within the community – individual as well as collective self-determination provide the base. Membership of the community can be acquired; one has to share the same political ideals and knowledge and create a fitting national identity. (Zimmer, 2003, pp.7). The crucial difference to the cultural nation is that all members of the community within a 'Staatsnation' commit themselves voluntarily to the nation. In England, the national consciousness which emerged through the establishment of the parliament mirrors this understanding; it was a community of will.

Liberalism and suffrage

Liberalism is defined as a movement implementing rationalism instead of religion as the base for governing. The liberal state aimed to guarantee specific individual rights based on reason. As long as these rights were given the individual subordinates its will to the public good and general will. One of the most important was the right of private property. Every individual had to have the right to accumulate as much property as one wants as well as being able to sell and buy freely. This lay the ground for the open and liberal financial market of modern times. The second important right was the protection of the individual from arbitrary and unfair treatment by the state. This could only be accomplished through the implementation of rule of law. One legal code which had to be valid for everyone in the same manner and before which, every citizen was treated equal. Opello highlights the importance of a liberalized legal system; "…the law should rule because it allows individuals the greatest freedom by protecting their private interests…" (Opello, 1999, p.96). In general, the liberal state should function to prevent absolutism. This is mirrored in the Act of Settlement, created after the Glorious Revolution. This Act forbade the instalment of monarchical absolutism in England.

John Stuart Mill argued that the greatest threat to liberty and the liberal system of the state lies in uneducated, irrational citizens who follow social norms without question. Consequently, a rational and well-educated citizenship would be the best guarantee for the liberal state to survive and flourish. Mill considered economic success as proof for rationality, this explains why in England the right to vote was at first restricted to the economically successful, property owning part of citizenship.(Opello, 1999, p.99). Several Reform Acts then expanded the voting community step by step, until in 1884 suffrage was granted too all male citizens of the country.

Conclusion

England distinguishes itself through; firstly having taken a gradually different path than other European entities. The absence of harsh forms of absolutism in combination with the early establishment of an operational parliament are among the most important factors, which make the English nation state building a special case within Europe.

Secondly, it was one of the first countries in Europe to complete the transition to a nation state:
Feudalism in England set the ground for the creation of a raw, early version of Parliament. However, one has to keep in mind that this form of Parliament still had a long way ahead to our known, modern version and only met the minimum requirements. Nevertheless, once it acquired supreme authority (at least next to the monarch), it furthermore suited the remaining characteristics for the sovereign state as defined by Roberts. That is to say, firstly the defined territory, which has been supported from the fact of being an island and having natural limitations. The authority was not held by a monarch, but by parliament. Consequently, the possibility of participation, which is included in the foundations of the concept, led to the result of being legitimized by the people. Parliament consisted mostly of the nobility, which in feudal times had financial as well as military power and was therefore able to enforce its decisions. These requirements were met already as early as in the thirteenth century.

Nation formation went hand in hand with state building. The English nation evolved through a more or less natural development rather than through an active construction as it is implied in the term nation 'building'. This was the case because England did not suffer from such extreme revolts against an oppressing, absolutist power to the same extent as other European nations, such as France. Therefore, the English defined their common culture over shared political ideologies and interests, in contrast to the significant invention of tradition which took place on the continent.

In conclusion, England can be defined as a political nation. These changes of state building and nation development occurred not exactly congruent, as their genuine peaks seem to be slightly shifted. Nevertheless, England took a pioneering role in its comparatively early manifestation as a unified and relatively modern nation state.

14

References

Braddick, M.J.
(1993).An English Military Revolution?
The Historical Journal , Vol. 36, No. 4 (Dec., 1993), pp. 965-975
Published by: Cambridge University Press

Craig, Gordon, & George, A.L.
(1990). *Force and Statecraft. Diplomatic Problems of our Time* (2nd ed.). New York:
Oxford UP.

Duffy, Maureen.
(2001). *England. The making of the myth from Stonehenge to Albert Square*. London:
Fourth Estate.

(Editor).
(1996). The Nation: real or imagined. The Warwick debates on nationalism. *Nations
and Nationalism*, 2, 3, pp. 357-370.

Gellner, Ernest.
(1983). *Nations and Nationalism*. Ithaca, NY: Cornell UP.

Gellner, Ernest.
(1994). Nationalism and Modernization & Nationalism and High Cultures. In:
John Hutchinson and Anthony Smith (Eds.). *Nationalism*. Oxford: Oxford
University Press

Hall, Stuart.
(1984). The State in Question. In G. McLennan & D. Held & S. Hall (Eds.), *The
Idea of the Modern State* (pp. 1-9). Milton Keynes: Open University.

Hobbes, Thomas. Leviathan. 1651

Kantorowicz, Ernst H.
(1957). *The king's two bodies: a study in mediaeval political theology*. Princeton, NJ:
Princeton University Press.

Kohn, Hans. The Genesis and Character of English Nationalism
Journal of the History of Ideas , Vol. 1, No. 1 (Jan., 1940), pp. 69-94
Published by: University of Pennsylvania Press
Article Stable URL: http://www.jstor.org/stable/2707011

Kumar, K.
(2003). *The making of English national identity*. Cambridge [etc.]: Cambridge University
Press

Maddison, Angus (2001). *The World Economy: A Millennial Perspective*. Organisation for
Economic Co-operation and Development. ISBN 92-64-18654-9.

Merriman, John
(1996). *A History of Modern Europe from the Renaissance to the Present*. New York, etc:

W.W. Norton & Company.

Opello, Walter C., & Rosow, Stephen J.(1999). *The Nation-State and Global Order. A Historical Introduction to Contemporary Politics.* London: Lynne Rienner.

Palmer, R.R., & Colton, Joel.
(1995). *A History of the Modern World* (8 ed.). New York: McGraw-Hill.

Parker, G. (1976). The 'Military Revolution' 1550-1660 - a Myth? *Journal of Modern History, 48,*
195-214.

Renan, Ernest. "What is a Nation?" in Eley, Geoff and Suny, Ronald Grigor, ed. 1996. Becoming National: A Reader. New York and Oxford: Oxford University Press, 1996

Schulze, H.
(1996). *States, Nations and Nationalism. From the Middle Ages to the Present.* Cambridge (USA):Blackwell Publishers Ltd.

Smith, Alan G. R.
(1997). *The emergence of a nation state: the commonwealth of England, 1529-1660* (2nd ed.). London [etc.]: Longman.

Lyly, John. The Complete Works of John Lyly
(1902). edited by R. Warwick Bond, Second Edition

Zimmer, Oliver.
(2003). *Nationalism in Europe, 1890-1914.* London: Palgrave MacMillan